COME
THIRSTY
PARTICIPANT'S GUIDE

COME THIRSTY

PARTICIPANT'S GUIDE

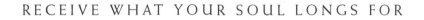

RECEIVE WHAT YOUR SOUL LONGS FOR

Based on the book by

MAX LUCADO

THOMAS NELSON
Since 1798

NASHVILLE DALLAS MEXICO CITY RIO DE JANEIRO BEIJING

Published in Nashville, Tennessee, by Thomas Nelson. Thomas Nelson is a trademark of Thomas Nelson, Inc.

Thomas Nelson, Inc. titles may be purchased in bulk for educational, business, fund-raising, or sales promotional use. For information, please e-mail SpecialMarkets@ thomasnelson.com.

ISBN 978-1-4185-3390-8

Printed in the United States of America

HB 02.12.2024

TABLE OF CONTENTS

*"Whoever drinks of the
water that I shall give
him will never thirst. But
the water that I shall give
him will become in him a
fountain of water springing up
into everlasting life."*

—John 4:14 NKJV

COME THIRSTY
READING PLAN

Week 1

♦ Read the Introduction of *Come Thirsty*. As you read through "Meagan," her story will sound strangely familiar. As this introduction unfolds, we discover a young woman who is thirsting for something real.

♦ Read Chapter 1 of *Come Thirsty*: "The Dehydrated Heart"—Unless we are drinking deeply at the well of God's supply, our hearts become dehydrated—dry, depleted, parched, and weak.

Week 2

♦ Chapter 2: "Sin Vaccination"—We were all born with a terminal disease—hopelessly infected by sin. See how God made a way for us to live disease free.

♦ Chapter 3: "When Grace Goes Deep"—Grace is a gift of God. Take a look at what happens when you try to put conditions on the grace of God. Grace is what defines us.

♦ Chapter 4: "When Death Becomes Birth"—Don't allow the dread of death to take away your joy of living.

● Chapter 5: "With Heart Headed Home"—We live caught between what is and what will be. Our hearts are longing for heaven, and every day that passes brings us closer to home.

Week 3

● Chapter 6: "Hope for Tuckered Town"—Some of us try to live our Christian lives completely in our own power. God offers hope for us when the effort wears us down.

● Chapter 7: "Waiting for Power"—Before we move forward, sometimes God asks us to wait . . . and pray.

● Chapter 8: "God's Body Glove"—The Holy Spirit works with us and through us, hand in glove.

● Chapter 9: "It's Not Up to You"—God paid too high a price for us to leave us unguarded. The Holy Spirit reminds us of our place in God's heart and comes to our aid in times of weakness.

Week 4

● Chapter 10: "In God We (Nearly) Trust"—We know that God knows what's best. We know that we don't. We also know that God cares, so we can trust him.

THE PRAYER OF
THE THIRSTY

Lord, I come thirsty. I come to drink, to receive.

I receive your work on the cross and in your resurrection.

My sins are pardoned and my death is defeated.

I receive your energy.

Empowered by your Holy Spirit, I can do all things

through Christ who gives me strength.

I receive your lordship. I belong to you.

Nothing comes to me that hasn't passed through you.

And I receive your love. Nothing can separate me from your love.

Amen.

INTRODUCTION

Who are we? Busy people. Burdened people. Burned-out people. Stained, stressed, and stretched people, longing for refreshment. These are all symptoms of a dryness deep within. A need. A thirsting. Deprive your soul of spiritual water and it will tell you. Dehydrated hearts send desperate messages. Snarling tempers. Waves of worry. Whispers of guilt and fear. Hopelessness. Sleeplessness. Loneliness. Resentment. Irritability. Insecurity. But God doesn't want us to live like this.

Like the woman at the well, we must recognize our need for living water. Our hearts are parched, dry, dehydrated. We need moisture, a swallow of water, a long, quenching drink. And where do we find water for the soul? "If anyone thirsts, let him come to Me and drink. He who believes in Me, as the Scripture has said, out of his heart will flow rivers of living water" (John 7:37–38 NKJV). Jesus invites: *Are your insides starting to shrivel? Drink me.* What H_2O can do for your body, Jesus can do for your heart. Come and see what the Lord can do in your heart! Come ready to receive the refreshment your soul longs for. Come, and come thirsty.

WELL

Receive Christ's Work on the cross.

Receive the Energy of his Spirit.

Receive his Lordship over your life.

Receive his unending, unfailing Love.

THIRSTING AFTER RIGHTEOUSNESS

Blessed are those who hunger and thirst for

righteousness, for they shall be filled.

—Matthew 5:6 NKJV

READ

Read the Introduction and Chapter 1 at home this week.

As you read through Meagan's story, it will sound strangely familiar. As this introduction unfolds, we discover a young woman who is thirsting for something real. And in Chapter 1 we discover that unless we are drinking deeply at the well of God's supply, our hearts become dehydrated—dry, depleted, parched, and weak.

⟨⟩ REFLECT ⟨⟩

**Answer the questions in this section at
home before your group discussion.**

Meagan is used to the whispers, the looks, the lines. She's
heard it all and done it all, and she's tired. Weary. Worn out.
She needs some relief from the constant "doing" without any
"accomplishing." She needs a savior. And in walks Jesse, the
quiet counselor from Alabama who pricks a nerve and gets her
thinking that maybe there's more to life than what she has.

♦ In this modern-day version of the story of the woman at
  the well (see John 4), we gain a new understanding of
  what that Samaritan woman would have been like, and
  the significance of Jesus' reaching out to her to change
  her life. What new thing did this story reveal to you?

♦ Where do you think the story goes from here? How does Meagan's life change as a result of her meeting Jesse? Do other lives change as well?

One crisp October morning in Jerusalem people had packed the streets, sleeping in tents and reenacting the rock-giving-water miracle of Moses. As the priests circled the altar seven times, pouring the symbolic liquid out, Jesus, the rustic rabbi from the northlands, stood up and called out. This was not a polite clearing of the throat; it was an attention-getting scream. "If anyone thirsts, let him come to Me and drink" (John 7:37 NKJV).

● Explore the significance of this action on Jesus' part. Look at it in context of the other discussions he's had about his divinity with the disciples. Have you recognized the importance of this declaration before?

What water can do for your body, Jesus can do for your heart. Water is a symbolic theme throughout the Scriptures. Ponder the importance of H_2O and its connection to the person of Jesus Christ and his lifesaving sacrifice on the cross. Consider the brown, tepid water lying stagnant in Hezekiah's well versus the constantly fresh, crystal-clear water flowing from the well of life. Start by looking up these verses and writing a sentence or two with your thoughts.

Genesis 1:2

Exodus 14

1 Kings 18:30–39

Psalm 23:2

Mark 1:9–11

Matthew 14:22–33

○ ⟨⟩ **DISCUSS** ⟨⟩ ○

Engage in conversation about these
questions within your small group.

Your Maker has wired you with thirst—a "low fluid indicator." Let your fluid level grow low, and watch the signals flare. Dry mouth. Thick tongue. Achy head. Weak knees. Deprive your body of necessary fluid, and your body will tell you.

♦ How does your body let you know you're running low on water, food, energy, and so forth?

Deprive your soul of spiritual water, and your soul will tell you. Dehydrated hearts send desperate messages. Snarling tempers. Waves of worry. Growling mastodons of guilt and fear. Hopelessness. Sleeplessness. Loneliness. Resentment. Irritability. Insecurity. These are warnings. Symptoms of a dryness deep within.

♦ How does your spirit let you know you're running low on God?

♦ Today, does your heart feel dried up? Shriveled?
   Dehydrated?

Meagan's story is a modern-day translation of the woman
at the well's story. Jesus (or Jesse) came to offer life-giving
water: himself. And the woman, Meagan, though jaded and
rough around the edges, softens in his presence and accepts the
powerful gift, remarkably without skepticism.

♦ What did you think of this retelling? Did it shed new
   light on a classic story for you? What similarities or
   differences from your own life stood out to you?

When we're running low on Jesus, our spirits let us know. Do you listen? Or do you ignore the warnings? Don't let your heart shrink into a raisin. Drink good water. Not everything you put your lips to will satisfy your thirst. The arms of a forbidden love can only satisfy you for a brief time. Eight-hour workweeks grant a sense of fulfillment, but never remove the thirst.

♦ So, where do you find water for your soul?

• Do you feel as though you have rivers of living water flowing from your heart?

Like water, Jesus goes where we can't. He seeps into the cracks of our lives, hydrating and "aquifying" our hearts. And, thankfully, we don't have to give him directions—just as we don't instruct water as it makes its way through our system. But so often we are tempted to instruct God on how he is to help us, nurture us, restore us. We tell him what we think we need.

● How do you find yourself instructing Jesus in your life?

● Discuss the difference between giving Jesus permission to work in your spirit and telling him what you think you need.

"If anyone thirsts, let him come to Me and drink." Literally, this is translated, "Let him come to me and keep drinking." One bottle won't satisfy. Ceaseless communion satisfies thirsty souls.

● Do you go to the well often? Or do you try to get by with drops from shallow puddles? (What would be an example of the "well" or "shallow puddles" in your life?)

● How do you engage in ceaseless communion? Why is this important?

WRAP UP

In the week ahead, return to the Prayer of the Thirsty (page xv) at least once a day. Set a time to commune with God intimately. Pray these words and meditate on their meaning in your real, day-to-day life. Journal in the space provided, and track any changes you notice in your spiritual energy level.

THIS WEEK'S PRAYER REQUESTS

MEMORY VERSE

Jesus stood and cried out, saying,
"If anyone thirsts, let him come to Me
and drink. He who believes in Me, as
the Scripture has said, out of his heart
will flow rivers of living water."

— John 7:37–38 NKJV

NOTES

NOTES

WELL

Receive Christ's Work on the cross.

GRACE BLOCKERS

For by grace you have been saved through faith,
and that not of yourselves; it is the gift of God.

—Ephesians 2:8 NKJV

READ

Read Chapters 2–5 this week.

This section of the book addresses the W in WELL—God's work on the cross and in Jesus' resurrection. Chapter 2, "Sin Vaccination," shows us that we are all born with a terminal disease; we are hopelessly infected by sin. See how God made a way for us to live disease free. Chapter 3, "When Grace Goes Deep," discusses grace as a gift of God. Take a look at what happens when you try to put conditions on the grace of God. Grace is what defines us. Chapter 4, "When Death Becomes Birth," warns us against allowing the dread of death to take away the joy of living. And Chapter 5, "With Heart Headed Home," tells us we live caught between what is and what will be. Our hearts are longing for heaven, and every day that passes brings us closer to home.

○ ☉ **REFLECT** ☉ ○

Answer the questions in this section at home before your group discussion.

The godless lead a *me*-dominated, childish life, a life of "doing what we felt like doing, when we felt like doing it" (Eph. 2:3 MSG). Take a look through Scripture and study *me* versus *we* in the Bible. Many people have fallen from great heights because of *I*—read their stories and write a sentence or two about the turning point toward self-centeredness in their lives.

Eve (Gen. 3)

David (2 Sam. 11)

Judas (Matt. 26:14–16)

Moses (Num. 20:6–12)

When our lives are wrecked by sin, we have only one salvation: Jesus. Not Muhammed or Moses or Buddha. What uniquely qualifies Jesus to safeguard the sin-sick (see 2 Cor. 5:21)?

Spend some time thinking about the different ways grace defines who you are. Reflect on Ephesians 2:4–9 for additional insight.

DISCUSS

Engage in conversation about these questions within your small group.

The sinful mind dismisses God. His counsel goes unconsulted. His opinion, unsolicited. His plan, unconsidered. The sin-infected grant God the same respect middle-schoolers give a substitute teacher—acknowledged, but not taken seriously. We pay a high price for such self-obsession. "God isn't pleased at being ignored" (Rom. 8:8 MSG).

◆ What is your image of God?

Just as flea-infested rats carried the bubonic plague through the villages of Europe, killing twenty-five million people, sin is a contagion that destroys souls.

◆ Discuss how our sins as individuals are as contagious as physical diseases. How do our actions affect and infect the people around us?

In the parable of the gracious father and the hostile brother (better known to us as "the parable of the prodigal son") we see the heavy burden of legalism. The older brother resolves to rain on the forgiveness parade. But for the little brother there are too many tasks. Keeping the robe spotless, the ring positioned, the sandals snug—who could meet such standards? Gift preservation begins to wear on the young man.

* How does gift preservation wear on you in your life? Be specific about the rules you feel compelled to follow.

* Do you expect there to be a "catch" to God's grace?

Grace-blockage runs rampant in our faith communities. In our hearts we feel that the Father may have let us in the gate, but we have to earn our places at the table. Or that God has made the down payment on our redemption, but we have to pay the monthly installments. But what good is grace if we cut it short, refuse to let it go deep? Deeply flowing grace clarifies, once and for all, who we are.

● How does God's grace define you?

● If you feel that God's grace does not define you, what then is your "label"?

Paul said in 1 Corinthians 15:10, "By the grace of God I am what I am" (NKJV).

● Discuss the freedom that comes from living in God's grace.

Solomon tell us that "the day you die is better than the day you are born" (Eccles. 7:1 NLT). This is certainly not the mind-set most of us have here on earth, yet in this portion of the book, heaven is described as a maternity ward with grandparents monitoring delivery-room doors.

● What is your idea of death and the afterlife? Do you think of it with positively glowing emotions or with fear and dread? Or do you simply ignore the uncertain future?

◆ Is your fear of dying robbing you of the joy of living?

"But we are citizens of heaven, where the Lord Jesus Christ lives. And we are eagerly waiting for him to return as our Savior" (Phil. 3:20 NLT). We read about the story of Lazarus in this section, and his submission to return to earth and live out his days in a vibrant demonstration of Jesus' lordship. He was enjoying the fruits of perfection in heaven, yet he came again to the fallen earth to serve his Master.

◆ What do you imagine the effect of Lazarus's return to earth was on his friends and family?

We've grown accustomed to the hard bunks and tin plates of an orphan in this world. Seldom do we peer over the fence into the world to come. It's been ages since we've shown someone our pictures of the adoptive Father coming to take us home. But the Scriptures tells us, "Friends, this world is not your home, so don't make yourselves cozy in it" (1 Peter 2:11 MSG).

◆ How have you made yourself cozy here in this life?

◆ What do you need to do to keep your heart headed toward home?

So how do we take regular ladle dips from the well of God's return? "Let heaven fill your thoughts. Do not think only about things down here on earth" (Col. 3:2 NLT). But what does that mean for us in "real life"?

- Discuss practical ways you can live like Carinette, the adopted orphan, and let your home-to-be dominate your thoughts.

WRAP UP

This week as you walk through life, pay attention to the grace blockers in your journey. And consider: are you placing grace blocks on yourself or others? Identify them. Then come to the well and take a long drink.

THIS WEEK'S PRAYER REQUESTS

○ ◌ MEMORY VERSE ◌ ○

For by grace you have been saved through faith, and that not of yourselves; it is the gift of God, not of works, lest anyone should boast. For we are His workmanship, created in Christ Jesus for good works, which God prepared beforehand that we should walk in them.

—Ephesians 2:8–10 NKJV

Notes

WELL

Receive the Energy of his Spirit.

REDEFINING PRAYER

"Not by might nor by power, but by
My Spirit," says the LORD of hosts.

—Zechariah 4:6 NKJV

READ

Read Chapters 6–9 at home this week.

This week focuses on the E in WELL—God's energy. In Chapter 6, "Hope for Tuckered Town," some of us try to live our Christian lives completely in our own power. But God offers hope for us when the effort wears us down. In Chapter 7, "Waiting for Power," we see that before we can move forward, sometimes God asks us to wait . . . and pray. In Chapter 8, "God's Body Glove," we learn how the Holy Spirit works with us and through us, hand in glove. And in Chapter 9, "It's Not Up to You," we explore the idea that God paid too high a price for us to leave us unguarded. The Holy Spirit reminds us of our place in God's heart and comes to our aid in times of weakness.

○ ◎ **REFLECT** ◎ ○

Answer the questions in this section at home before your group discussion.

Citizens of Tuckered Town turn the key, start the car, slip it into neutral, and lean in to shove! The Corinthian Christians pushed a few cars too. They believed that by doing their own work they were pleasing God more.

◆ Does "pushing your car" make you more spiritual? Look at 1 Corinthians 3:1–3 and Galatians 3:3; 5:16 for further insight.

While we wait for God, we should wait with other believers. Scripture tells us, "Live with [others] in an understanding way. . . . Do this so that nothing will stop your prayers" (1 Peter 3:7).

◆ What does the phrase "that nothing will stop your prayers" mean?

◆ Compare that thought to 1 John 5:14 and 1 Peter 3:12.

Consider the illustration of a hand in a glove to bring clarity to God's working in our lives. We become the glove, and he is the hand moving within us. "I myself no longer live, but Christ lives in me" (Gal. 2:20 NLT). But the process comes slowly.

- Think (and write a few sentences) about why some people walk with such confidence while others stumble with such regularity. Consider the lives of important figures in the Bible when you answer.

Much of the discussion this week centers on the work and role of the Holy Spirit in our lives. Holy Spirit discussions lead us into the realm of the supernatural and unseen. Often we grow quickly quiet and cautious, fearing what we can't see or explain.

♦ Journal about your perception of the Holy Spirit. Is he a familiar friend to you, or is he a strange and confusing concept? Having an honest understanding about the way you approach the Holy Spirit will help you in the group discussion later.

DISCUSS

Engage in conversation about these questions within your small group.

Life in Tuckered Town is unappealing, tiresome, and petty. No one in his right mind would want to live there. Yet that is often the picture we present—through our actions—to those on the brink of turning to Christ. All they see are harsh words, joyless days, contentious relationships, and thirsty hearts. Nothing repels non-Christians more than gloomy Christians.

♦ Has this been true in your experience—from either side of the fence?

Consider the statement, "I used to think there were two kinds of people: the saved and the unsaved. Paul corrects me by describing a third: the saved, but unspiritual." The spiritual person relies wholeheartedly on the Spirit for his energy; he seeks to "walk in the Spirit" (Gal. 5:16 NKJV).

♦ What does it mean to be saved but unspiritual? Does that concept contradict your sensibilities?

"If you are thirsty, come to me!" Jesus declares. "If you believe in me, come and drink!" (see John 7:37–38). Come to me, he says. Not come to my church or come to my system, but come to *me*. Come to me and drink.

- What do you feel compelled to "come to"? What outside pressures have been put on you to conform to preexisting notions or traditions?

God's Spirit rages within you; whether you feel him or not is unimportant. Jesus said, "Living water will flow out from within" (John 7:38 NLT) and "a spring of water [is] gushing up inside" (John 4:14).

♦ Do you feel this living water in you? Or do you feel weary and irritable?

♦ What should we do when we don't feel the living water and instead have the compassion of Hermann Goering, can't stand our mothers, or can't forgive ourselves (see Eph. 5:8)?

In the early days of the church, as many as 120 souls huddled in the same house to meet for worship. How many potential conflicts existed within that group? Did some glare at Peter for denying Christ at the fire? Others complained that the women were there—this should be a men's meeting! And on and on. Yet they persisted. They continued to gather. And the Holy Spirit visited them—a great reward for their dedication.

♦ Surely there are conflicts among the faithful today as well. What keeps you from wanting to meet in worship?

It is so hard for us to wait for God. Who has time to wait? We groan at the thought of such *inactivity*. But waiting on God is hardly that. It is watching for him. Looking for his power. Anticipating his move.

◆ Why do you find it hard to wait on God?

◆ Where in your life do you need to wait for him? The bus stop of new love? The mailbox of career change?

The idea of praying constantly or being vigilant in prayer sounds burdensome to us. It leaves us wondering, *My business needs attention, my children need dinner, my bills need paying. How can I stay in a place of prayer?* Change your definition of *prayer.*

- What is your definition of *prayer?* How does it need changing?

A theme in this section about God's energy focuses on the question "How can the Spirit have more of me?" not "How can I have more of the Spirit?" C. S. Lewis put it well: "Give me All. . . . Hand over the whole natural self, all the desires which you think innocent as well as the desires you think wicked—the whole outfit. I will give you a new self instead."[1]

---

1 C. S. Lewis, *Mere Christianity* (New York: MacMillan Publishing Co., 1952), 167.

♦ As you look around your life, what are your areas of resistance? Remembering the story about the cat trapped in the attic but not released (page 75), what "varmints" of the soul have you trapped but forgotten to release?

Some of you need to sit down. You fly furiously back and forth, ever busy, always thinking the success of this journey is up to you. You need to receive Christ's energy and let go into his perfect rest.

♦ Do you fear letting up? Do you fear slowing down?

"The Spirit himself joins with our spirits to say we are God's children" (Rom. 8:16). What an intriguing statement. Deep within you, God's Spirit confirms with your spirit that you belong to him. Beneath the vitals of the heart, God's Spirit whispers, "You are mine. I bought you and sealed you, and no one can take you."

⬥ When, if ever, did you first hear this whisper in your heart? How do you keep that voice fresh as a reminder of your role in this universe?

Do you have any idea that your needs are being described in heaven, just as the Florida pastor was lobbying for help for his friend with AIDS at a White House briefing? The Holy Spirit "prays for us with groanings that cannot be expressed in words. And the Father who knows all hearts knows what the Spirit is saying, for the Spirit pleads for us believers in harmony with God's own will" (Rom. 8:26–27 NLT).

◆ What is happening in your life today that you need the Holy Spirit to take to the Father for you?

◆ Do you feel pressured to say the right thing when you bring your requests to God, or do you find comfort in the fact that the Holy Spirit makes our requests known to God on our behalf? Or both?

WRAP UP

Revisit the Prayer of the Thirsty again this week, and claim Christ's energy as your own. Make a point of developing your awareness of him as you go through your days, thinking of him and talking to him constantly.

THIS WEEK'S PRAYER REQUESTS

MEMORY VERSE

*Let us therefore come boldly to the throne
of grace, that we may obtain mercy
and find grace to help in time of need.*

—Hebrews 4:16 NKJV

NOTES

Notes

WELL

Receive his Lordship over your life.

CHOOSING PEACE

*"You cannot add any time to your
life by worrying about it."*

—Matthew 6:27

READ

Read Chapters 10–13 at home this week.

This week focuses on the first L in WELL—God's lordship. Chapter 10, "In God We (Nearly) Trust," reminds us that we know that God knows what's best and we don't. We also know that God cares, so we can trust him. In Chapter 11, "Worry? You Don't Have To," we see that worry changes nothing and only shows us that we aren't trusting God to do as he promised. Chapter 12, "Angels Watching over You," shows that when we accept God's lordship in our lives, we can be assured that many mighty angels will guard us in all our ways. And in Chapter 13, "With God as Your Guardian," we are told that God closely guards those who turn to him.

⟨⟩ REFLECT ⟨⟩

Answer the questions in this section at home before your group discussion.

No leaf falls without God's knowledge. No dolphin gives birth without his permission. No wave crashes on the shore apart from his calculation. God has never been surprised. Not once.

⬥ Meditate on God's lordship. Do you acknowledge it in your life? Do you know it's best for you? The following verses can help inform your thoughts:

Psalm 115:3

Isaiah 43:13

Isaiah 46:10

Ephesians 1:11

John 19:11

Acts 2:23

Lamentations 3:37

Paul wrote to the Christians at Philippi and told them not to worry, despite the fact that they were being attacked from every angle. Do a little exploration into their circumstances. What were their emotional struggles? What were real, tangible threats?

- Write a few sentences about the state of the church in Philippi to gain a better understanding of where they were coming from. Can you think of modern examples of these pressures? (See Phil. 1:15–17; 3:2–3, 18–19; 4:2, 19.)

Biblical and contemporary pictures of angels don't match up. Grocery store tabloids present angels as Thumbelina fairies with see-through wings. They exist to do us favors. They are heaven's version of bottled genies who find parking places and lost keys.

♦ What does the Bible say about angels (see Deut. 33:2; 2 Kings 6:17; Ps. 68:17; 103:20; Matt. 26:53; 2 Thess. 1:7; Heb. 12:22; Rev. 5:11)?

♦ What is your current level of self-worth? Do you picture yourself as one who warrants God's oversight?

♦ Read Psalm 91 and journal on God's perspective of you.

DISCUSS

**Engage in conversation about these
questions within your small group.**

The immediate problem we encounter when we approach the lordship of Christ is the existence of evil. How can a good God allow bad things to happen? If God cares, he isn't strong; if he is strong, he doesn't care. He can't be both.

- Discuss the problem of evil. How do you reconcile God's lordship with the presence of sin in our lives? Why do people struggle?

Heaven does not ask, "How can I make you happy?" God may use blessings. Then again, he may use buffetings. Both belong to him.

● How does this make you feel? Does it make you angry, offended, comforted, or secure? Is this easy or hard for you to accept?

"In this world you will have trouble," the Bible warns (John 16:33). God did not spare even his Son from pain on this earth. The glory of God outranked the comfort of Christ.

● When you think about the fact that Christ also suffered to bring glory to his Father, does that change your perspective on what you've been discussing?

♦ Have you been called to endure a "Gethsemane season"?

A word of caution: the doctrine of sovereignty challenges us. Study it gradually. Don't share it capriciously. When someone you know faces adversity, don't insensitively declare, "God is in control." A cavalier tone can eclipse the right truth. Be careful.

♦ What is an appropriate response to someone in pain?

You don't add one day to your life or one bit of life to your day by worrying. Your anxiety earns you heartburn, nothing more.

♦ How often do you worry? To what extremes?

♦ Worry, which betrays a fragile faith, can be thought of as a kind of unintentional sin. How is this true (or untrue) in your life?

When you worry, you're not managing your problems; you're letting your problems manage you. The worrisome heart pays a high price for doing so.

♦ How is worrying not only "not helpful" but also counterproductive—making your situation even worse?

Your Father in heaven knows the kind of characters—the giant of abuse, the dragon of layoffs, the ogre of broken relationships—that may come into your life. The only way to overcome worry is to stay close to Christ.

♦ What does it mean, in a practical sense, to stay close to Christ?

The promise of angelic protection is limited to those who trust God. Refuse God at the risk of an unguarded back. But receive his lordship and be assured that many mighty angels will guard you in all your ways.

♦ Does God's protection allow you to be more bold in your life? Are you free to take more risks than you would otherwise?

♦ When you think of God's lordship, does it feel like a loss of control, or do you see the perks that come with being a child of God?

On one dark and brooding afternoon, a remarkable act of self-sacrifice took place. The role model in this situation—a bird. Sitting near the side of the road, a mother bird was exposed to the rain, her wing extended over her baby who had fallen out of the nest. The fierce storm prohibited her from returning to the tree, so she covered her offspring until the wind passed.

♦ From what winds is God protecting you?

The silversmith places an ingot of silver on an anvil and pounds it with a sledgehammer. Once the metal is flat, into the fire it goes. The worker alternately heats and pounds the metal until it takes the shape of a tool he can use. Heating, pounding. Heating, pounding. Deadlines, traffic. Arguments, disrespect. Heating, pounding.

● What are the forces of heating and pounding that are especially effective in your life? What are those outside elements that turn you back to God every time?

WRAP UP

Perhaps one of the best ways to celebrate God's amazing love and grace is to share some of that love and grace with others. Who in your life—family member, co-worker, neighbor, fellow church member—most needs encouragement right now? Think of a special, maybe even unusual, way to show God's love to that person.

THIS WEEK'S PRAYER REQUESTS

⟨⟩ **MEMORY VERSE** ⟨⟩

*Be anxious for nothing, but in everything
by prayer and supplication, with
thanksgiving, let your requests be made
known to God; and the peace of God, which
surpasses all understanding, will guard your
hearts and minds through Christ Jesus.*

—Philippians 4:6–7 NKJV

NOTES

WELL

Receive his unending, unfailing Love.

ABIDING IN GOD'S LOVE

*"As the Father loved Me, I also have
loved you; abide in My love."*

—John 15:9 NKJV

READ

Read Chapters 14–16 at home this week.

This week focuses on the final L in WELL—God's endless love for us. In Chapter 14, "Going Deep," we plunge into the depths of the limitless love of God. In Chapter 15, "Have You Heard the Clanging Door?" we see that some fear they've gone too far, done too much, wandered too long to be worthy of God's love. But the God who knows everything about you loves you still. And in Chapter 16, "Fearlessly Facing Eternity," we are reminded that God knows our imperfections, yet he has chosen us. We need never fear God's judgment. Trust his love.

○ ◌ **REFLECT** ◌ ○

Answer the questions in this section at home before your group discussion.

The mystery of the deep calls the deep-water free diver. He wants to go deeper. Let's go on a similar descent into the limitless love of God. Read Ephesians 3:17–19 and journal about God's undying love for you.

It's easy to believe that success and health are signs of God's love, and that addiction and tragedy are signs that he has forgotten us. But what does Scripture have to say about that? Look into the lives of the following giants of the faith and consider the circumstances of their lives in relation to God's love for them. What trials did they endure; what blessings did they receive?

David

Job

Mary, the mother of Jesus

John

Rahab

Eli

How deep is God's love for you? Read Romans 8:38–39 and journal a response to what Paul says about the depths of God's love. Consider any favorite hymns or other spiritual writing that may reflect God's love for his children.

Take a look at what the Bible has to say about Judgment Day. What should your attitude be in approaching the end of this life? What do we know to be true, and what is just vain imaginings? (Read Ecclesiastes 3:17; Matthew 25:41; John 5:22; Romans 2:2; Hebrews 9:26–28; 1 John 4:17–18; and Revelation 19:1–3 for additional insight.)

○ ◇ **DISCUSS** ◇ ○

**Engage in conversation about these
questions within your small group.**

The sight of the healthy or successful prompts us to
conclude, *God must really love him. He's so blessed with health, money,
good looks, and skill.* Or we gravitate to the other extreme. Lonely
and frail in the hospital bed, we deduce, *God does not love me. How
could he? Look at me.*

- Do you find that you often measure God's love by
  outward signs, temporary measuring sticks?

For anyone desiring a descent into God's love, Scripture
offers us an anchor: "God is love" (1 John 4:16). This verse
surrounds us, liberates us, and covers us with the undying
affection of our heavenly Father.

♦ How does God show his love to you? When do you most feel loved by God?

When you abide somewhere, you live there. You grow familiar with the surroundings. You don't consult the blueprint to find the kitchen. To abide is to be at home.

♦ What does abiding in Christ mean to you? How does that look in your everyday life?

Anhydrobiosis: life without water. When drought hits, the roundworm curls up, shuts down, and waits for water to come to it. Scientists assure us that humans can't do this. But we've seen plenty of anhydrobiosis of the heart, haven't we? The wife who left her husband and kids after twenty years of marriage. The man who murdered his estranged family. The neighbor with a debilitating addiction.

* How do you withdraw from things when your spirit gets dehydrated?

* We were not made to live this way, so what can we do to avoid it?

Do you feel incarcerated? Not in a jail, but by personal guilt and shame? No need to request mercy; the account is empty. Make no appeal for grace; the check will bounce. You've gone too far. The tragedy is that if we aren't convinced of God's love and grace then we can't convince others.

- Do you fear you've "gone too far" in life? How have you "sold out" to win God's affection or the affection of others?

- How do you reassure yourself of God's love for you?

On the night of Jesus' crucifixion, when the Romans appeared, the followers disappeared in a blur of knees and elbows. Those mighty men, who are seen today on stained-glass windows in a thousand cathedrals, spent the night crawling beneath donkeys and hiding in haystacks. But Jesus came back to them. They outran the guards, but they couldn't outrun the love of Christ.

- Do you feel you have ever lived a "loveless day," when God did not love you?

- Describe a time in your life when you turned your back on Jesus, but he still loved you.

Judgment Day. The phrase alone is enough to cause the toughest linebacker in the NFL to tremble in his cleats. We know God hates sin. We know he sees all sin. And we know we have sinned—a lot. It's hardly a comforting thought. But Scripture promises that we can face God with confidence on the Day of Judgment. Why? Perfect love expels all fear (see 1 John 4:18).

◆ Do you need some fear expulsion in your life?

◆ Does the idea of Judgment Day give you anxiety?

"Whom have I in heaven but you? And earth has nothing I desire besides you. My flesh and my heart may fail, but God is the strength of my heart and my portion forever" (Ps. 73:25–26 NIV). "My heart has heard you say, 'Come and talk with me, O my people.' And my heart responds, 'Lord, I am coming'" (Ps. 27:8 TLB).

- Does your heart respond as the psalmist's does? What does that look like in your life?

WRAP UP

God promises that even if we are faithless, he will remain faithful. To help you remember his love for you, try this exercise, which may make you a little uncomfortable. Sit down and make a catalog of the specific ways you believe you may have failed your Lord in the last year. After you have finished your list, give God joyful thanks for his forgiveness. Then burn your list!

THIS WEEK'S PRAYER REQUESTS

MEMORY VERSE

Yes, I am sure that neither death, nor life, nor angels, nor ruling spirits, nothing now, nothing in the future, no powers, nothing above us, nothing below us, nor anything else in the whole world will ever be able to separate us from the love of God that is in Christ Jesus our Lord.

—Romans 8:38–39

Notes

WELL

Receive Christ's Work on the cross.

Receive the Energy of his Spirit.

Receive his Lordship over your life.

Receive his unending, unfailing Love.

IF GOD WROTE YOU A LETTER

The LORD will guide you continually, and
satisfy your soul in drought, and strengthen your
bones; you shall be like a watered garden, and
like a spring of water, whose waters do not fail.

—Isaiah 58:11 NKJV

READ

Read Chapter 17 at home this week.

Chapter 17, "If God Wrote You a Letter," imagines what a personal letter from God would read like.

○ ⟨⟩ REFLECT ⟨⟩ ○

Answer the questions in this section at home before your group discussion.

Do some exploring through the Bible. Pick your favorite verse or verses that apply to each aspect of WELL—God's work, energy, lordship, and love.

○ ⟨⟩ DISCUSS ⟨⟩ ○

Engage in conversation about these questions within your small group.

The children of San Salvador receive Christmas packages and letters from a far-off place. But were no one to tell them to open the boxes, they would carry the box to their dirt-floored home, place it in a prime location, admire it, and display it, but never open it. Don't we do the same with Christ? Aren't we prone to keep him at arm's length?

♦ In what ways do you keep Christ displayed, yet unopened, in your life? Why?

The associates of Lawrence of Arabia came to Paris and discovered indoor plumbing. But they were sorely mistaken in the source. Lawrence caught them, wrenches in hand, dismantling the faucets to take back home with them so they could "have all the water they want."

* Through what faucets has God poured his love into your life?

* Have you responded the same way these men from Arabia did—by putting your focus on the faucet rather than the unending spring of water?

In this study we've discussed a lot about the fact that life, pain, struggle, glory, joy, and success are not about us, but about God. He is the treasure. The reward is not the gift, but the Giver.

- Why is it so easy for our hearts to be captured by the gifts of God rather than God himself?

- What do you value most about the Giver?

Over the last six weeks, you've discussed exciting truths about God's work on your behalf and for his own glory, God's energy feeding your soul, God's lordship in your life, and God's unending love for you.

♦ What concept has most impacted your faith or changed your way of thinking?

WRAP UP

If you could write a letter to God that could be delivered this very day, what would you say in that letter? Take some time to write that letter—of thanks, of praise, of petition, or whatever you would like to say in such a special note—and then offer it to God. Keep the letter in a safe and special place and revisit it later, especially on dark and difficult days, so you can say along with the psalmist, "I am still confident of this: I will see the goodness of the LORD in the land of the living" (Ps. 27:13 NIV).

THIS WEEK'S PRAYER REQUESTS

MEMORY VERSE

The LORD *will guide you continually,*
and satisfy your soul in drought, and
strengthen your bones; you shall be
like a watered garden, and like a spring
of water, whose waters do not fail.

—Isaiah 58:11 NKJV

NOTES

NOTES

You don't have to live with a dehydrated heart. God invites you to treat your thirsty soul as you would treat your physical thirst. Just visit the WELL and drink deeply:

> Receive Christ's **work** on the cross,
> The **energy** of his Spirit,
> His **lordship** over your life,
> And his unending, unfailing **love**.
> Come thirsty, and drink the water of **life**.

$14.99
ISBN 978-0-8499-1404-1

Published by
THOMAS NELSON™
Since 1798
www.thomasnelson.com

MAX LUCADO

3:16

A STUDY
FOR
SMALL
GROUPS

If 9/11 are the numbers of terror and despair, then 3:16 are the numbers of hope. Best-selling author Max Lucado leads readers through a word-by-word study of John 3:16, the passage that he calls the "Hope Diamond" of scripture. The study includes 12 lessons that are designed to work with both the trade book and the Indelible DVD for a multi-media experience.

Listen to the message of 3:16 in your home or take it on the road. This CD makes the perfect gift for the family or friends you want to hear the hope found in John 3:16.

MAX LUCADO

NEW YORK TIMES BEST-SELLING AUTHOR

3:16

THE
NUMBERS
OF HOPE

MAX LUCADO

AUTOR DE ÉXITOS DE LIBRERÍA DEL NEW YORK TIMES

3:16

LOS
NÚMEROS
DE LA
ESPERANZA

3:16 is also available in Spanish, Portuguese, German, Swedish, Dutch, Korean, Japanese, and Chinese.

GOD'S GREAT BIG LOVE FOR ME

With colored beads built right in, this board book is the perfect book to teach the verse and meaning behind John 3:16 to preschool children.
Available February 2008

3:16 – THE NUMBERS OF HOPE
TEEN EDITION

Max offers his unique and simple storytelling for this important message while Tricia Goyer writes teen responses to Max's message, guiding teens to fully understand how this verse can impact their lives. From confession to praise, these responses are sure to bring an insightful look into the personal faith of teens.
Available February 2008

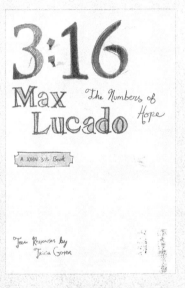

A DVD FOR SMALL GROUP STUDY

This is a kit designed and priced specifically for small groups. It will include a copy of the study guide for small groups, an evangelism booklet, the Indelible DVD, and a CD-ROM with facilitator's guide information and promotional material.